For my mom and dad, who when I
was small agreed to slow the car down "so I
could see everything." Merry Christmas!

UNIVERSE

NEW YORK ✦ CHRISTMAS

PHOTOGRAPHY BY MARK CROSBY

First published in the United States of America
in 1999 by

UNIVERSE PUBLISHING
A Division of Rizzoli International Publications, Inc.
300 Park Avenue South
New York, NY 10010

Distributed in the U.S. trade by
St. Martin's Press, New York
Distributed in Canada by McClelland and Stewart

99 00 01 02 03/10 9 8 7 6 5 4 3 2 1

Printed in Singapore

Design by Amelia Costigan

*Towering over Midtown, the Citicorp
building looks ready to lift off with
holiday spirit.*

by Hugh Martin

foreword

I am a Californian. Worse than that, I'm a Southern Californian. But before I became one, I was a New Yorker. Looking at Mark Crosby's evocative photographs of that implausible metropolis, I became one again. Just like that. Only took a few magical moments. Amazing what one man with a touch of genius can do, given a never-before-and-never-again city and a camera.

We all, I think, tend to dream occasionally of being happy little bluebirds flying over the rainbow, though the destinations we crave are as varied as we are. When I was a child, I was not tempted by Oz — or Camelot or Alice's Wonderland. Nor, as I slid into adulthood, by Shangri-La or Bali Hai. No, I wanted to go to New York — not when I died, NOW, if we could pack fast enough! Why? Because I had a young Southern Belle mother who was possessed by New York mania. So, in 1920, when I was old enough for travel (about six), she took me there where I, too, became as infatuated with New York (if not more so) as my crazy mother. She may have been crazy, but she was marvelous company; what glorious times we had, especially at Christmastime. Oz seemed elementary compared to R. H. Macy. I ran wild in the toy department and raced up the "Down" escalators and down the "Up" escalators, blithely scattering shoppers left and right until thwarted by the house security. (We didn't have escalators in Birmingham, Alabama.)

There was no Christmas tree at Rockefeller Plaza then, probably because there was no Rockefeller Plaza, but who needed it when I could sleigh ride in Central Park and feed squirrels in the snow? The Salvation Army rang bells and gave us live brass bands. Come to think of it, everything was live then. Amplified music, synthesizers, and worst of all, muzak, were mercifully missing from the urban scene.

And what a scene it was! The store windows — Lord & Taylor, Saks Fifth Avenue, Bergdorf Goodman, Bonwit Teller, and best of all, Tiffany, were bursting with opulence and fantasy. Oh, and F.A.O. Schwarz! What a playing field for a six-year-old boy with a tendency (already) to hedonism!

What is so miraculous about New York — especially at Christmastime — is that the magic never fades. If anything, it becomes more and more like a fairytale. And that boy who reveled in it all was still reveling when he got to be sixty, seventy, even eighty!

I never would have dreamed that such enchantment could be caught and frozen on clean white pages in a beautiful book. But Mark Crosby is an alchemist, and alchemists can do things like that. Look at his carved lion guarding the New York Public Library; he is as proud — and seemingly not a day older — as he was in 1920 when I, wearing knickers, climbed all over him. Behold the majestic nave of St. Patrick's Cathedral.

Who needs Oz? I'm almost tempted to say "Who needs Heaven?" (Only kidding, Lord!) The way Crosby has shot it, I can almost smell the incense and feel the warmth of the candles close to my frozen fingers. And it's good to see Bloomingdale's, too. My very first job in Manhattan was delivering mail to various departments in that illustrious store. It was more elegant then, before all the psychedelic lights and salesgirls dressed in short skirts right up to here!

And thank you, Mark, for conjuring up for me once more New York's glorious bridges — and street lamps — and churches — and trees — and the embellishments on the old mansions. Your camera has convinced me that they look even more beautiful in the rain and fog and snow.

I wish you weren't too young to have captured the old Metropolitan Opera House, or the gorgeous Empire Theater, especially its interior, before they destroyed these two noble landmarks. But Lincoln Center has a certain nouveau riche charm; and there are still some pretty theaters to be found. New York *is* theater, isn't it? The whole thing is theater! Your book is theater, too. Every time I open it, I can almost hear the overture. And I feel as if I'm about to be led to a seat in the tenth row center by a Radio City Music Hall usher in full regalia.

So thank you for these superb photographs. Because of them, each year on my birthday, faced with an ever-increasing number of candles, I will no longer find myself wishing I were six again. I can just drink in the beauty of your impressions of Babylon-on-the-Hudson and there it is again: the wondrous joy of being a child in New York.

Hugh Martin may be the last of the Golden Age popular songwriters. He is best known for the musical score to Meet Me in St. Louis *(starring Judy Garland), which includes his timeless and beloved, "Have Yourself a Merry Little Christmas." In addition to his visit in 1920, Mr. Martin lived in New York from 1933 to 1974.*

A trio of wreaths hangs in the Fifth Avenue courtyard of The Frick Collection. The Frick marks
the southern end of "Museum Mile," a stretch of
Fifth Avenue that also includes The Metropolitan
Museum of Art and the Guggenheim musuem.

by Mark Crosby

preface

A little over three years ago, a big snow
storm hit New York City. What began
almost unnoticed by busy New Yorkers quickly
turned into a blinding blizzard. And though the
clatter and rumble of snow-chained salt trucks
and plows would be heard through the night, it soon
became apparent to all that nothing would be open the following day, and a holiday was in store for the whole of the city.

The next morning a winter sun broke onto a cityscape transformed.
Gone were the traffic noises that typify New York's frenetic thorough-
fares. Gone were the dark grays of its canyons. In their place stood a New
York of yesteryear, with dazzling white vistas and nothing but the sound
of wind and human voices. Streets and avenues — even Fifth Avenue —
were born again as trampled snow paths for bundled pedestrians and
cross-country skiers. And the air was crisp and smelled of wood smoke
curling from brownstone fireplaces.

It was early January that year, and though Christmas and New Year's had passed, holiday lights and ornaments still decorated shop windows and townhouse doorways. For photographers like me, it was a moment not to be missed, and judging by the ranks of amateur and professional picture-takers fanning out that next morning, the event would be well recorded.

A few days later, with a more familiar New York back in place and rid of its snow (much of it gathered onto barges and taken out to sea), I went looking for a book of photographs of New York at Christmas thinking it would be fun to own one. To my complete surprise, none could be found. There was no such book in print, I was told. No Christmas book?! New York!? Home for more than sixty years to both the Rockefeller tree and the Radio City Christmas Spectacular?! The same place where each Thanksgiving for four generations a Macy's parade has welcomed Santa? Even the author of " 'Twas the Night Before Christmas" once called New York home. Here then was an irresistible opportunity.

Three years and too many photographs later, I am delighted to say that you now hold in your hands the book I had once hoped to find. I say this because its images confirm that New York is indeed the wonderfully inspiring and serendipitous place it is known to be at Christmas. And since (unlike a snowfall) this book did not happen overnight, I wish to thank by name the many who helped bring it to pass.

Deepest thanks go to my mom and dad, to my brothers Glenn, Scott, and Andrew, and to their wives, Liz, Elizabeth, and Molly, and to the

Rev. Thomas K. Tewell, for their sustaining interest, encouragement, and support. Thanks also in this regard go to my friends Chris Browder, Danny Fetterman, Rob Johnston, Jim Higgason, Anne and Hampton Sides, Sloan Harris, Mike King, Mark Lencke, Mary Tabor Engel, Janet Willemain, Joe Cuticoni, Kevin Cole, David Russell, Stanford Brent, Bob Goldstone, Richard Hershenson, Seth Rose, Peter Hite, Kevin McKiernan, Mike Mumper, and Bruce Mandelbaum.

For technical and creative input that help define many images in this book, I am grateful for the wonderfully talented photographers Steve Burns, Frederick Charles, Stephanie Badini, Erik Pendzich, and Maggie Hopp. And for helping me summit Rockefeller Center for the lighting of the tree, or wedge myself into dusty, hundred-year-old crawl spaces of the Cathedral of St. John the Divine (while twelve stories below Handel's Messiah rang out in full measure), thanks go to Cindy Yoder, Elisabeth Pearson, Holly Gonzales, and the Rev. Elizabeth Wheeler.

Thanks finally to Hugh Martin for his wonderful introduction, and to Universe Publishing, particularly its Publisher, Charles Miers, for taking on the project. And to my editor, Abigail Wilentz, and the book's designer, Amelia Costigan, whose talent and enthusiasm have found their way onto every page. And, now, if I may borrow a few words from that famous New Yorker of a century past, "Happy Christmas to all, and to all a good night!"

N.Y.C. TAXI

4N81

An icy-cold East River flows silently between Brooklyn's River Café and lower Manhattan's Financial District.

ABOVE: *Looking more like a visitor from another planet than from the North Pole, Santa spreads a little Christmas cheer along Fifth Avenue, Cadillac style.*

PAGE 17: *With no other reference than the majestic (and very French-looking) Ansonia — one of the oldest apartment buildings on the Upper West Side — these lights appear to be strung along the Champs Élysées rather than on Broadway.*

fifth Avenue, in short, looked just as Fifth Avenue is supposed to look a week or so before Christmas. Even the air, cold and smelling of automobile exhaust, the Arctic and roasting peanuts, was as it should be. The people, old and young, strolling the street were as well. To look at their faces was to see every country on earth — and maybe a few beyond it.

—Editorial Page, *The New York Times*

December 18, 1993

The entrance to a West Village brownstone invites those who pass to reflect upon Christmas.

ABOVE: *Patience, who along with Fortitude, guards the entrance to The New York Public Library on 42nd Street, bears a holiday wreath with noblesse oblige.*

RIGHT: *Each year, Cartier's huge red bow wraps the biggest gift in town; the jeweler acquired this Renaissance mansion in 1917 in exchange for a pearl necklace.*

Looking more like the Star in the East than a snowflake, Fifth Avenue and 57th Street's so-called "Tiffany Snowflake" (since Tiffany stands on the southwest corner) guides wisemen to a girl's best friend.

PAGE 24: *Redolent with saffron bouill-*
abaisse and bustling with purposeful
waiters, Balthazar restaurant, at Crosby
and Spring Streets, makes for a perfect
holiday destination when SoHo shopping
gets to be too much (provided, of course,
you made reservations).

PAGE 25: *Vesuvio, family owned for over*
eighty years, tempts holiday passersby
with breads and pastries so fresh they
steam the bakery's window.

Freshly fallen snow provides a momen-
tary canopy for The Mall, in Central
Park. Fondly known as Literary Walk,
the passage is adorned with statues of
such legendary figures as Byron, Shake-
speare, and Sir Walter Scott.

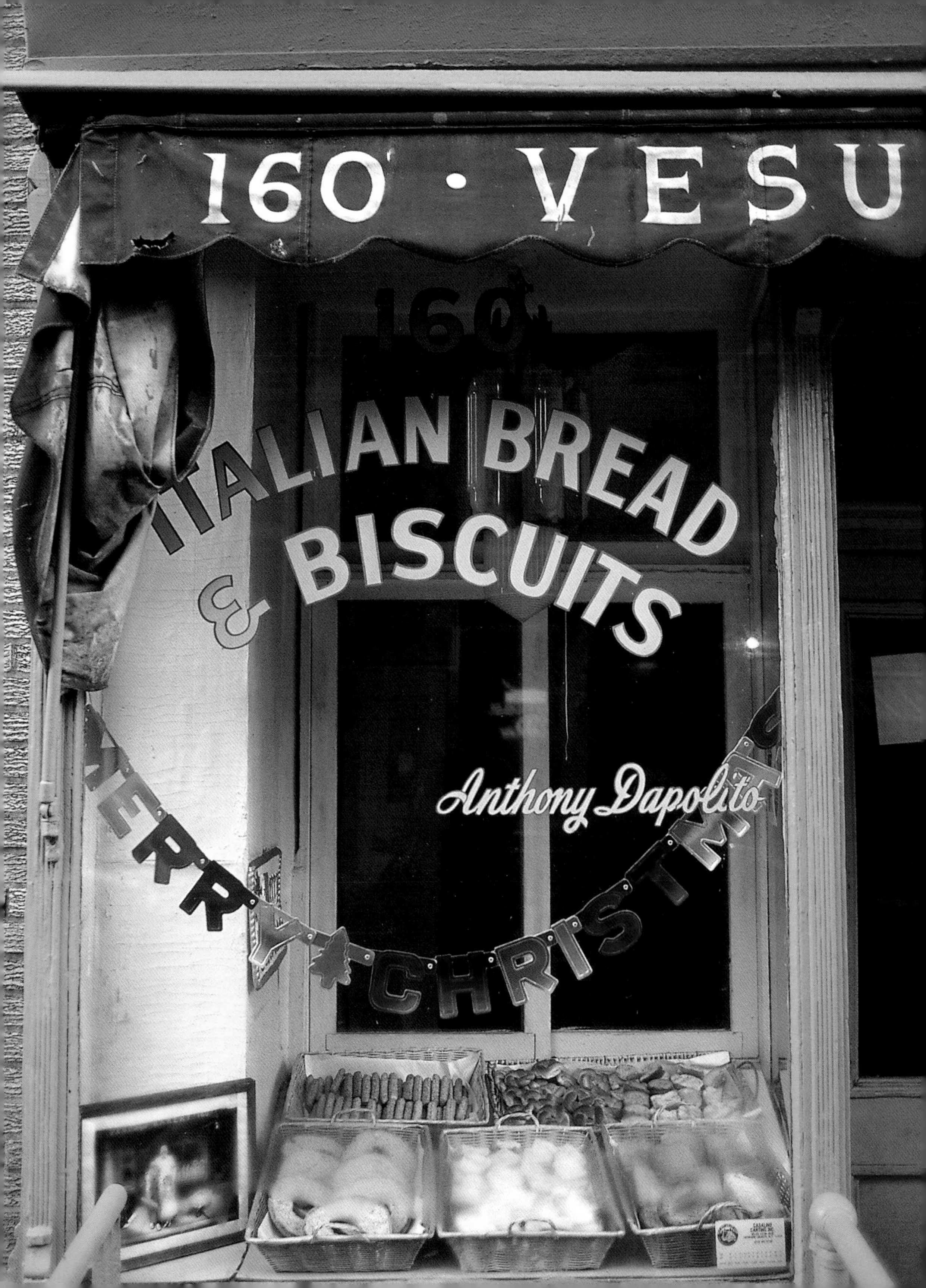
160 · VESU
160
ITALIAN BREAD
& BISCUITS
Anthony Dapolito
MERRY CHRISTMA

*As the youngest of Rockefeller Center's
featured skaters, Kelly O'Grady prepares
to skate before a very large audience — the
tree-lighting and pageant leading up to it
are broadcast across the nation.*

i am eight years old. Some of my little friends say there is no Santa Claus. Papa says, "If you see it in *The Sun*, it's so." Please tell me the truth, is there a Santa Claus?

—Virginia O'Hanlon, Letter to the Editor,
The New York Sun, 1897

… Yes, Virginia, there is a Santa Claus. He exists as certainly as love and generosity and devotion exist, and you know that they abound and give to your life its highest beauty and joy. Alas! How dreary would be the world if there were no Santa Claus! It would be as dreary as if there were no Virginias….

— Editorial Page, *The New York Sun*, 1897

Crowds gather to view the Christmas windows of Saks Fifth Avenue, an annual tradition since 1924.

"When out on the fire escape there arose such a clatter; I threw open my dead-bolted window guards to see what was the matter."

ABOVE: *Nearly 200 performances of the*
Radio City Christmas Spectacular *each*
season confirm that the show, which opened
in 1933 — a year after the Music Hall opened
— remains as popular as ever. As always,
the Rockettes take center stage.

LEFT: *There's no business like "snow"*
business, and these Rockettes show why!

PAGE 30: *A pint-sized Santa peers out from*
the second-story window of a West Village
apartment building.

The newly fallen snow atop these Upper West Side brownstone stoops looks more like the work of a pastry chef than of Mother Nature.

Christmas greenery, at a coffee beanery, makes this Upper West Side café a perfect holiday stop.

The multicolored lights at Barney's, a bastion of chic, are outshown by the over-the-top window displays.

In remembrance of those New York City residents who gave their lives in
the service of our country, two-and-a-half miles of lighted trees have decorated
Park Avenue every Christmas since 1945. Following the playing of Taps by a U.S.
Army Band trumpeter on the steps of the Brick Presbyterian Church at 91st
Street and Park Avenue, the memorial trees are lit all at once on the first Sunday
evening in December. The Helmsley Building's twelve-story lighted cross has
commemorated these sailors and airmen since 1952.

How could the startled wise men

Find their way

Beneath these clusters

Of Electric stars?

In stables here

No meadow-scented hay

Is piled where shepherds

Might kneel down to pray;

Between these rows

Of huge horn-throated cars

There is no room

For softly stirring sheep,

Sweet drowsy oxen

Or a child asleep.

— Jean Batchelor, "Manhattan Christmas"

The New Yorker, December 21, 1929

ABOVE: *A wreath — made of baskets of cinnamon, orange peel, cloves, and allspice — hangs from the top of the four-story, Lalique-windowed atrium, welcoming visitors to Henri Bendel on Fifth Avenue.*

PAGE 40: *With the Rockefeller tree directly across Fifth Avenue from its main entrances, Saks Fifth Avenue can convincingly claim to be ground zero for Christmas shoppers.*

PAGE 41: *A red child's dress adds a festive touch to holiday garland in the windows of Bonpoint, a children's clothing boutique on Madison Avenue.*

The Metropolitan Museum of Art displays its matchless, seventeenth-century Neapolitan Crèche every December for visitors.

Traditional Christmas decorations adorn brownstones along St. Luke's Place in the West Village.

The cast-iron scroll work of the Apthorp's West End Avenue entrance shows up beautifully with a fresh touch of snow.

ABOVE: *Pedestrians enveloped by a winter storm fleetingly compose a Victorian tableau outside the gates and courtyard of the Apthorp apartment building on the Upper West Side.*

RAISING OF THE CHRISTMAS TREE: *From its humble Depression-era origin, when workmen put up a small tree amidst the muddy construction site that was to become Rockefeller Center, the tree-lighting and the skating pageant that precedes it have become a national event enjoyed by millions. Today, the tree boasts over twenty-six thousand lights and five miles of wire, requiring nearly three weeks of preparations before the tree is lit in early December.*

OPPOSITE: *Although the size and type of tree vary over the years, this ninety-foot Norwegian spruce, hoisted into place at Rockefeller Center in mid-November, was by far the year's largest Christmas tree in the country.*

Live Christmas trees take up temporary residence in the Grand Army Plaza, just outside the Fifth Avenue entrance to the Plaza Hotel.

m anhattan has been compelled to expand skyward because of the absence of any other direction in which to grow. This, more than any other thing, is responsible for its physical majesty. It is to the nation what the white church spire is to the village — the visible symbol of aspiration and faith, the white plume saying that the way is up.

— from E. B. White, *Here Is New York*, 1949

As viewed from the wooden promenade
of Brooklyn Bridge, midtown Manhattan's
singular skyline makes clear to all that
Christmas is in full gear.

St. Patrick Cathedral's symmetrical setting was not always there. When built, shortly after the Civil War, the cathedral was considered so far out of town that half its parishioners failed to attend services.

The New York Fire Department doesn't find St. Patrick's request for a little holiday help too "unwreathonable."

Carolers congregate among the columns of St. Patrick's main nave to sing "Silent Night."

Here, amid the quiet calm of newly fallen snow, there is little to remind one of the bustling city that surrounds this Central Park view.

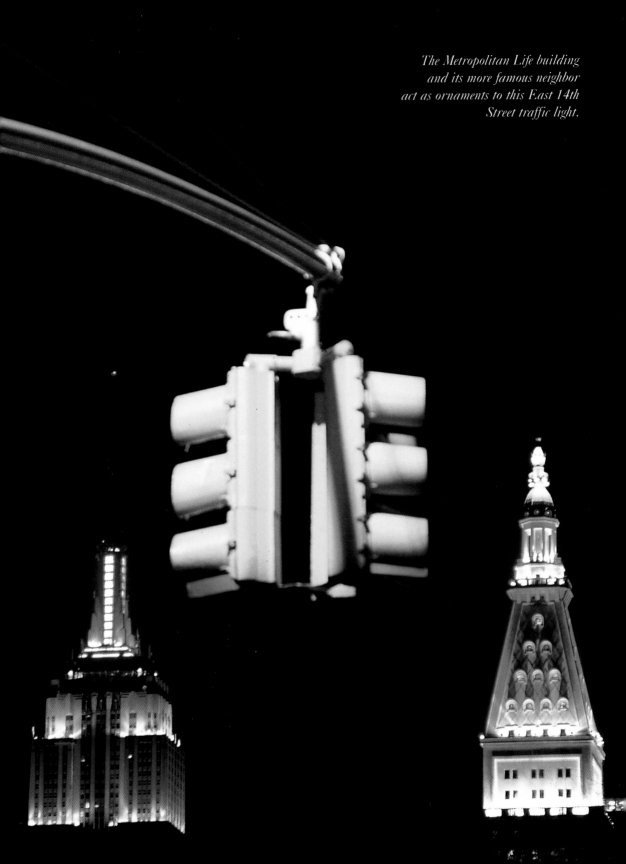

The Metropolitan Life building and its more famous neighbor act as ornaments to this East 14th Street traffic light.

t is December that is New York's month for people of all ages. The lights are a big part of it. Because night comes in mid-afternoon at this season, long before quitting time, the office towers blaze with light. The beauty of that light may be deepened by the New Yorker's subconscious sense of living in an oceanic city at the edge of the cold gray, scary Atlantic, destroyer of Titanics.

— Russell Baker, Editorial Page
The New York Times, December 9, 1997

Battling a driving December rain, this traveler appears unaware of the spun-gold that lights the way along Central Park West.

A king-size snowflake is led past the
American Museum of Natural History
by a Macy's helper in the superstore's
Thanksgiving Day Parade. Since
1924, the parade has marked the start
of New York's Christmas season.

Beneath the familiar facade of the Flat Iron Building, a lone Christmas Tree presides over Madison Square.

ABOVE: *Workers gathered at a window of One Rockefeller Plaza for the tree-lighting have their backs to an even bigger Christmas display.*

LEFT: *Prometheus silently presides over the Rockefeller Rink. The tree, not yet lit for the season, is directly overhead.*

Every Christmas, the origami tree at the American Museum of Natural History provides the best "paper-view" in town.

have yourself a merry little Christmas/ let your heart be light/ From now on our troubles will be out of sight.

Have yourself a merry little Christmas/ make the yuletide gay/ From now on our troubles will be miles away.

Here we are as in olden days/ happy golden days of yore/ Faithful friends who are dear to us/ gather near to us, once more.

Through the years we all will be together/ if the Fates allow/ Hang a shining star upon the highest bough, and have yourself a merry little Christmas now.

— "Have Yourself a Merry Little Christmas"
by Hugh Martin, 1943

ABOVE: *Myriad lights from Tavern on the Green cast this outlying lantern and wreath in silhouette. Each December, the restaurant fields more than 10,000 reservation requests a week.*

RIGHT: *Santa salutes morning shoppers from Cartier's Fifth Avenue balcony.*

Every winter, hoteliers, restaurateurs and shop-keepers wrap miniature lights around countless trees, such as these along West 57th Street, turning nearly all of Midtown's streets and avenues into enchanting promenades.

PAGE 76: *A pair of evergreens marks the entrance to a snow-covered Strawberry Fields in Central Park; the pair of towers behind them are atop the San Remo apartment building on Central Park West.*

PAGE 77: *It's 6:30 P.M. at Grand Central Terminal: time to head home for the holidays. Every day, through the portals of this Beaux-Arts masterpiece bestriding Park Avenue in Midtown, tens of thousands of people make their way to and from points Upstate.*

As the day's last light gives way to an early winter's night, galleries within the Metropolitan Museum of Art remain aglow.

Bloomingdale's makes it clear to all passersby that
serious shopping "B"-gins here. The store's first-day
sales, in 1872, totaled $3.68.

RIGHT: *Dressed in holiday garb, Polo's primary residence
is only one of many matchless sights along Madison
Avenue at Christmas.*

Santa and his helpers, en route to their temporary residence at Macy's, pause beneath the Beresford on Central Park West before heading down Broadway, to the delight of countless thousands along the way.

i 'm a nut for lightning- and snow-storms, and I stood at the window for what must have been half an hour, watching the big flakes whirl past the glass, watching Central Park turn into an etching as the black branches loaded up with white, watching the humps and depressions that marked paths and streets level off and disappear.

— Jack Finney from *Time and Again*

A red light can't stop the snow from falling on these trees along Columbus Avenue on the Upper West Side.

This New York resident is always delighted to learn of snow in the forecast. Gus (13 years old) and Lily (12) have lived at the Central Park Zoo since 1988.

Midtown's snow-shrouded skyline looks like distant mountains when viewed across the frozen expanse of Central Park's Boat Pond.

*On this rain-swept, wintry night,
these Upper West Siders have
found a safe harbor in Puccini's
Café on Columbus Avenue.*

Formal fountains and The Metropolitan Opera's Chagall paintings set the stage for Lincoln Center's Christmas tree.

A handbell choir is viewed from the triforium of the Riverside Church during its annual festival of carols. Speaking of bells, the church tower houses (on five floors) the world's largest carillon.

At the close of the Riverside Church festival of carols, a flame is passed from one candle to the next, gradually illuminating the beautiful, stone-vaulted ceiling high over head.

City sidewalks, busy sidewalks/ Dressed in holiday style/ In the air there's a feeling of Christmas/ Children laughing, people passing/ Meeting smile after smile/ And on every street corner you hear:

Silver Bells, silver bells/ It's Christmastime in the City/ Ring-aling, hear them ring/ Soon it will be Christmas day.

— "Silver Bells" by Jay Livingston and Ray Evans, 1950

LEFT: *The largest store in the world on one of the busiest days of the year.*

FOLLOWING PAGE: *Like a lonely sentinel, this tree guards the all-quiet entrance of a Sutton Place brownstone at dawn. In the distance is the Queensboro Bridge, elegant in any season.*